color
DESIGNS FOR LIVING

COLOR DESIGNS FOR LIVING®

Senior Editor: Vicki Ingham
Contributing Project Editors/Writers:
   Amber Dawn Barz, Jan Soults Walker
Contributing Writer: Jody Garlock
Contributing Graphic Designer: On-Purpos, Inc.
Copy Chief: Terri Fredrickson
Publishing Operations Manager: Karen Schirm
Senior Editor, Asset and Information Manager: Phillip Morgan
Edit and Design Coordinator: Mary Lee Gavin
Editorial and Design Assistant: Renee E. McAtee
Book Production Managers: Pam Kvitne, Marjorie J.
   Schenkelberg, Rick von Holdt, Mark Weaver
Contributing Copy Editor: Nancy Evans
Contributing Proofreaders: Tom Blackett, Julie Cahalan,
   Mary Helen Schiltz
Contributing Indexer: Stephanie Reymann

Meredith® Books

Executive Director, Editorial: Gregory H. Kayko
Executive Director, Design: Matt Strelecki
Managing Editor: Amy Tincher-Durik
Executive Editor/Group Manager: Benjamin W. Allen
Senior Associate Design Director: Tom Wegner
Marketing Product Manager: Brent Wiersma
National Marketing Manager-Home Depot: Suzy Johnson

Publisher and Editor in Chief: James D. Blume
Editorial Director: Linda Raglan Cunningham
Executive Director, New Business Development: Todd M. Davis
Director, Sales-Home Depot: Robb Morris
Executive Director, Sales: Ken Zagor
Director, Operations: George A. Susral
Director, Production: Douglas M. Johnston
Director, Marketing: Amy Nichols
Business Director: Jim Leonard
Vice President and General Manager: Douglas J. Guendel

Meredith Publishing Group

President: Jack Griffin
Senior Vice President: Karla Jeffries

Meredith Corporation

Chairman of the Board: William T. Kerr
President and Chief Executive Officer: Stephen M. Lacy
In Memoriam: E.T. Meredith III (1933–2003)

The Home Depot®

Marketing Manager: Tom Sattler

Note to the Reader: Due to differing conditions, tools, and individual skills, Meredith Corporation and The Home Depot® assume no responsibility for any damages, injuries suffered, or losses incurred as a result of attempting to replicate any of the home improvement ideas portrayed or otherwise following any of the information published in this book. Before beginning any project, including any home improvement project, review the instructions carefully and thoroughly to ensure that you or your contractor, if applicable, can properly complete the project, and, if any doubts or questions remain, consult local experts or authorities. Because codes and regulations vary greatly, you should always check with authorities to ensure that your project complies with all applicable local codes and regulations. Always read and observe all of the safety precautions provided by any tool or equipment manufacturer, and follow all accepted safety procedures.

We are dedicated to providing inspiring, accurate, and helpful do-it-yourself information. We welcome your comments about improving this book and ideas for other books we might offer to home improvement enthusiasts. Contact us by any of these methods:
Leave a voice message at: 800/678-2093
Write to:
Meredith Books, Home Depot Books
1716 Locust St.
Des Moines, IA 50309–3023
Send e-mail to: hi123@mdp.com

contents

how to use this book

From the pale peach of the sunrise to the deep navy of the night sky, life is filled with color. Color lifts the spirit, soothes the soul, and makes each day memorable. This book makes it easy to choose the perfect color schemes for your home interiors and offers advice on how to transfer these colors to the walls and surfaces that surround you every day.

Say goodbye to the guesswork of selecting color for your home. From finding color inspiration to deciding where to put each hue, you'll find the answers here. The designers and associates at The Home Depot® have put together a collection of colorfully decorated rooms in one easy-to-use book. *Color Designs for Living* will inspire you with hundreds of photographs and innovative ideas to create the ideal design to complement your tastes and lifestyle.

Whether you intend to decorate all or part of your home interiors yourself or plan to use the services of a professional designer or consultant, you'll need this resource for ideas and inspiration. For your decorating ease this book is divided into seven inspirational chapters:

GETTING STARTED. Two of the most common color dilemmas are determining with what colors you can live and which colors work well together in a room. Finding an existing inspiration is a nearly foolproof means for finding these answers. This chapter also explains how you can use the color wheel to find the perfect combination.

TIMELESS COMBINATIONS. If you want to decorate your home with color that never goes out of style, choose one of these classic combinations.

STYLE. Whether you prefer traditional, contemporary, or something in between, one of these color combinations will work beautifully with your decorating style.

TRENDS. These trendy color schemes show how exciting and up-to-the-minute color can be.

HOME TOURS. Take a tour of these attractive and inspiring whole houses to learn how to create color continuity within rooms and from room to room.

ROOMS. Attractive color solutions for every room in the home are featured here, including kitchens and bathrooms.

QUICK COLOR CHANGES. If you prefer color without commitment, or if you want to be able to change your color scheme often, this chapter is filled with easy-change color ideas.

getting
started

Whether you are most comfortable in surroundings filled with lively, vibrant hues or serene neutrals, a color scheme exists that's right for you. If you love color but others in your home are not comfortable with it, there's a scheme of compromises for you too. What you need first is the inspiration to get you started.

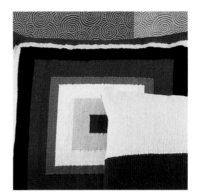

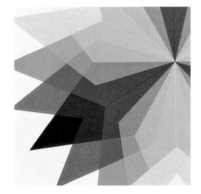

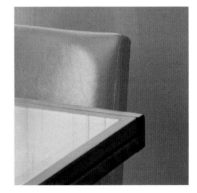

inspiration:
toss pillow

BEAUTIFUL BEGINNINGS. Somewhere under the rainbow is that one color or magical mix of hues that will make your room pop, sizzle, or soothe.

The question is, where will you find it? Starting with an inspiration piece, such as a fabric or a painting, filled with the colors you love gives you a head start because the fabric designer or artist has already done the color matching for you.

The inspiration piece becomes the foundation for your entire scheme. For example, you can use the fabric's background color as the wall color, the fabric's next most prominent color as your main upholstery fabric color, and the remaining accent colors for your accessories. Can't find a fabric you really like? Look in your closet. If you see lots of blue, for example, use it as the anchor for your scheme, or choose a scarf or tie that contains that favorite shade and use the remaining colors in the scarf on furnishings and accessories.

CONNECTING COLOR (ABOVE) Keeping colors in neighboring rooms closely related gives each room a slightly different feel—energizing in the family room *opposite*, inviting in the living room *above*—yet provides a seamless flow. Here, sunny yellow walls feel warm and welcoming while softer upholstery colors lend an air of relaxation.

STORAGE (ABOVE) Choosing paint colors should be one of the last decisions you make in decorating a room from scratch, because it's easy to have paint custom mixed to match any object or fabric. This handpainted chest boasts every color found in the inspiration pillow *below.*

AREA RUG (RIGHT) The gold-green stripe of the pillow is a close match to the gold-green tones in this area rug. For advice on mixing and matching analogous colors, see page 29.

TOSS PILLOW (LEFT) This toss pillow not only provided the inspiration for the colors used on the handpainted chest *above,* it also sparked selection of the entire room's upholstery and accessories.

UPHOLSTERY (ABOVE) The sofa's warm yellow-orange upholstery fabric matches one of the stripes in the bold patterned toss pillow.

FABRIC STORE (LEFT) This stack of fabric is part of a collection found at a nationwide fabric store chain. Look for similarly inspiring collections at a fabric store near you.

DEFINING FABRIC (ABOVE)
This contemporary print is the defining fabric for the living room decorating scheme; it contains nearly all of the shades found in the other fabrics.

WALL COLOR (BELOW) Another stripe from the fabric print defined the room's sunny yellow wall color. To ensure a perfect match, take your fabric to the home center paint department and have a sales associate custom mix the shade.

ACCESSORIES (LEFT)
Accessory colors, including the funky lamp and flower-filled vase, all blend with the shades found in the defining fabric.

TABLETOP PALETTE (ABOVE)
This soft, soothing scheme was created using the colors found in a simple table linen.

inspiration: table linens

LINEN SCHEME. The soft colors found in the floral print tablecloth define the color palette used in the dining room.

The background color of the tablecloth is almost the same as the color on the walls. To make the ceiling molding, window trim, and cabinetry stand out, a slightly darker shade of paint was used. The hues in the printed bouquets are repeated on the plaid chair covers. The gold tones are picked up by the print frames hanging on the wall and gold-rimmed dishes stacked inside the glass-fronted cabinetry. The palette continues on to the window seat pad and toss pillows and in the alabaster glass of the chandelier. The area rug echoes the deepest color found in the tablecloth.

The result is a soothing environment perfect for hosting everything from formal gatherings to casual, family friendly affairs.

TOP TO BOTTOM (ABOVE) From the alabaster glass of the chandelier shade to the fresh floral centerpiece, every color used in this room can be found in the tablecloth.

inspiration: rug

BLUE HUES. If you own the perfect rug, use it as the inspiration for your room's overall color scheme.

A blue striped rug inspired the intense blue, gray, and white design scheme of this gathering room. To make a room with a simple color palette interesting and exciting, combine the colors with plenty of pattern and texture. Here a wide-stripe nylon rug adds panache underfoot while graphic brushed-cotton pillows bring a punch of contrast to the solid-color gray sofa. If you can't find the perfect color in a purchased pillow, make your own using a pillow form (available at fabric stores) and a yard of fabric.

Add interest to the walls with embossed wallpapers as shown. Here different shades of blue form wide wall stripes. Cutouts in the wallpaper make way for a large portion of blue painted wall, which serves as a frame for white-matted photos.

COLOR PRINCIPLE

(RIGHT) This living room uses a bold blue, white, and gray scheme for easy, economical impact. Brilliant blue walls, large geometric patterns, and clean-lined accessories are simple and stylish.

FABRIC LONGEVITY

(LEFT) To keep upholstery fabrics looking crisp and new longer, spray them with a fabric stain guard and reserve white or light-color fabrics for pieces that get the least amount of use.

ROMAN SHADE (LEFT) The
colors in the striped fabric
shade spread to nearly every
surface in the room. Only the
wood plank floor, white-painted
woodwork, and a few wooden
furnishings remain neutral.

inspiration: window treatment

ROMAN SHADE. The citrus colors of the window shade *left* spread to the walls, cabinetry, upholstery, and accessories in this room, creating a gathering space that is both cheerful and bold. The vibrant fabric selections are key to this casual, upbeat look.

PATTERN PLAY. For major upholstered pieces stick to solid colors or subtle, small-scale patterns; this makes the pieces more versatile when it comes to mixing and matching. Add more color and patterns in smaller doses for variety and balance.

Tabletop accessories and wall art offer easy ways to infuse more color. Texture plays a part too. For example the flaking paint of the coffee table contrasts nicely with the smooth finishes on the rest of the wooden pieces. That element of contrast injects the variety that makes a room interesting.

Change scale too. In this room an oversize houndstooth check is a playful reference to the smaller-scale check on the armchair and window seat cushions.

All the fabrics feature a color from the striped Roman shade:

This pale green fabric covers the sofa.

This cheerful coral fabric covers several accent pillows.

This bright yellow paint was used on the walls.

Lime-green paint coats the built-in cabinetry.

This houndstooth print covers the armchair.

WINDOWS AND BACKSPLASHES

(ABOVE) Sheer window treatments and tumbled-marble wall tiles pick up the warm tangerine tones of the pottery displayed in this kitchen. Displayed on open shelves the pottery serves as a decorative focal point.

WALLS (RIGHT) A pale shade of green coats the walls of this kitchen. Dark chocolate brown contrasts with the brightly colored dishes in the open shelf display.

CABINETRY (ABOVE) The deepest green in the pottery inspired the cabinetry finish.

inspiration: dishware

GREAT GLAZES. If you love the colors found in a piece of pottery or a colorful vase, use the piece to define the colors in a room. In this kitchen dishware and serving pieces inspired the wall color, tile selection, and cabinetry finish.

GOOF-PROOF COLOR. If you are uncertain how big each dose of color should be, use a 60-30-10 formula as a guide. According to this formula, a predominant color should cover 60 percent of the room (usually the painted walls, or in the case of a kitchen, the majority of the cabinetry). A secondary color covers 30 percent of the room (window treatments, upholstery, rugs, and in kitchens, often the walls), while accent colors account for the remaining 10 percent of the items in the room (artwork, accent tiles, and accessories).

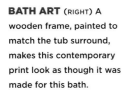

BATH ART (RIGHT) A wooden frame, painted to match the tub surround, makes this contemporary print look as though it was made for this bath.

inspiration: tile

LIGHT AND DARK. Even a countertop or floor tile can inspire the color scheme of a room. A simple pattern of white and dark chocolate floor tiles inspired the surface selections in this bath. The white tile of the flooring extends to the walls, while the deep chocolate tone of the tiles extends to the vanities, tub base, and freestanding storage cabinets.

The two tones are also picked up in the stonelike pattern of the quartz countertop.

The bath's dramatic focus is an art print featuring the same dark brown and white tones accented by warm rusts and khakis. For advice on choosing accent colors see "The Color Wheel" on pages 22–33.

VANITIES (LEFT) Open shelves on the vanity bases prevent the dark wood color from looking too heavy.

FLOOR TILE (RIGHT) Set in a basket-weave pattern, white tiles frame brown ones that have a shiny metallic finish.

SHOWER A glass shower makes the bath feel more open and spacious. A mocha brown bamboo ladder, which serves as a towel holder, sports a paler shade of brown.

PURE AND BRIGHT A primary palette of red, yellow, and blue makes for a cheerful, family-friendly room.

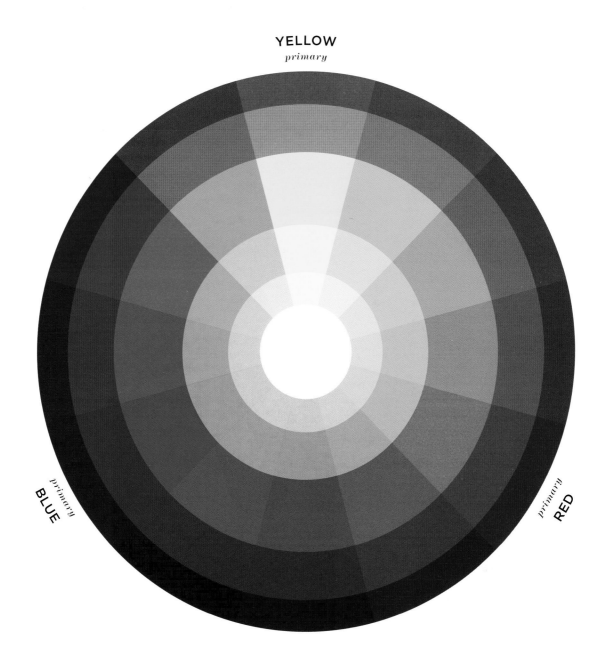

YELLOW
primary

primary
BLUE

primary
RED

the color wheel

CLASSIC INSPIRATION. Color has its own vocabulary. By learning the few simple terms discussed here and on pages 24–32, you can use the color wheel to help plan the perfect color scheme.

The color wheel offers several ways to find an attractive color palette. Start with a single favorite and work with schemes based on the groupings of primary, secondary, tertiary, analogous, complementary, and monochromatic.

PRIMARY. If you love vibrant hues, consider using classic primary colors— red, yellow, and blue. Each is a pure color that can't be created by mixing other hues. Choose your favorite of the three and balance it with wood tones and neutral accents, or pair any two of these colors together. For an even stronger color statement, combine all three; they work well with any decorating style.

BASIC COLOR WHEEL (ABOVE) The color wheel provides an easy way to see how hues relate to each other. Red, yellow, and blue are the primary colors from which other colors are mixed.

Like primary colors, secondary
colors work well together.
This bold orange dining area
provides warm contrast against
the cool earthy greens of the
chairs and the rug pattern.

SECONDARY (BELOW) A secondary color is created by mixing together two primary colors.

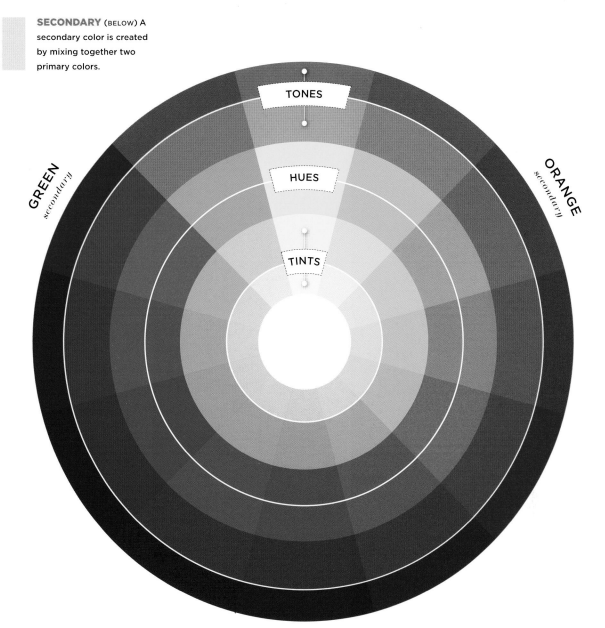

GREEN
secondary

ORANGE
secondary

TONES

HUES

TINTS

secondary
PURPLE

SECONDARY. The secondary colors are orange, green, and purple. Green comes from combining blue and yellow, orange from mixing yellow and red, and purple from blending red and blue.

Like primary colors secondary colors work well together. If you can't envision your room filled with a bold orange and green, pair up their paler tints (lighter values) of peach and sage or deeper tones (darker values) of terra-cotta and olive.

TINTS AND TONES COLOR WHEEL (ABOVE) This variation of a color wheel shows the pure hues (the third ring from the center) and some of the tints (the first and second rings) and tones (the fourth and fifth rings) of these colors.

HOT KITCHEN The tertiary colors of yellow-green, yellow-orange, and red-orange make this kitchen feel cheerful and inviting.

TERTIARY. These colors are created by mixing a primary color with its closest secondary color. The six tertiary colors are blue-green, yellow-green, yellow-orange, red-orange, red-purple, and blue-purple.

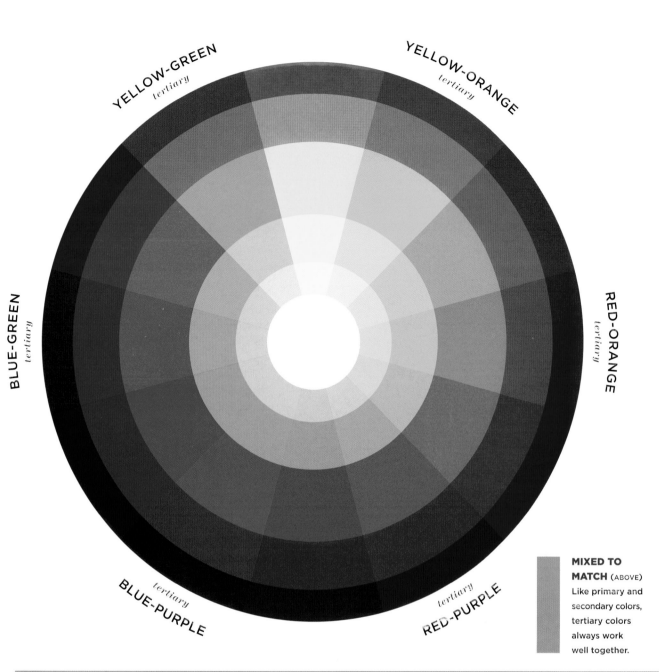

YELLOW-GREEN
tertiary

YELLOW-ORANGE
tertiary

BLUE-GREEN
tertiary

RED-ORANGE
tertiary

tertiary
BLUE-PURPLE

tertiary
RED-PURPLE

MIXED TO MATCH (ABOVE) Like primary and secondary colors, tertiary colors always work well together.

color basics

▸ **HUE** is a color's name, such as red, yellow, green, or blue.

▸ **VALUE** is the relative lightness or darkness of a hue. Lighter colors have added white; darker colors have added black.

▸ **CHROMA**, also known as saturation, is the intensity of a color, which is determined by how much gray is added to it. The primary colors—red, yellow, and blue—are pure colors with intense chroma.

▸ **TINTS** are colors that have been mixed with white, such as pastels.

▸ **TONE AND SHADE** refer to colors that have been mixed with black, such as brick red.

ANALOGOUS WARMTH
Warm up your kitchen or
any room in your home
with yellow, yellow-orange,
and orange. These colors
encourage conversation
and an optimistic attitude.

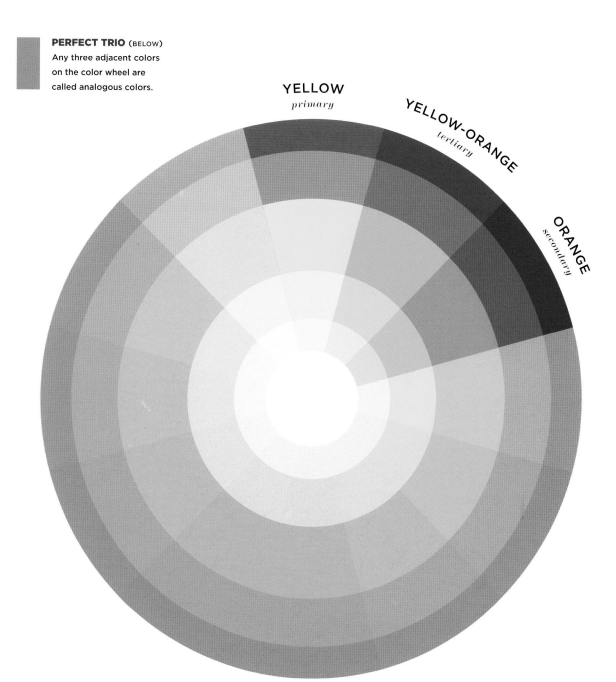

YELLOW
primary

YELLOW-ORANGE
tertiary

ORANGE
secondary

ANALOGOUS. Analogous colors are colors that lie next to each other on the color wheel. For example blue-green, green, and green-yellow are analogous colors. Because these adjacent colors share a component color, they always look good together. The analogous colors of yellow, yellow-orange, and orange create a lively, upbeat ambience in the kitchen.

EXACT OPPOSITES Orange and blue, opposites on the color wheel, make this kitchen appear bright and cheerful.

MOST ATTRACTIVE OPPOSITES
(BELOW) Generally, complementary
colors look best when they are
roughly equal in intensity and value.
Match pale tints with pale tints and
deep tones with deep tones so that
the hues are in balance.

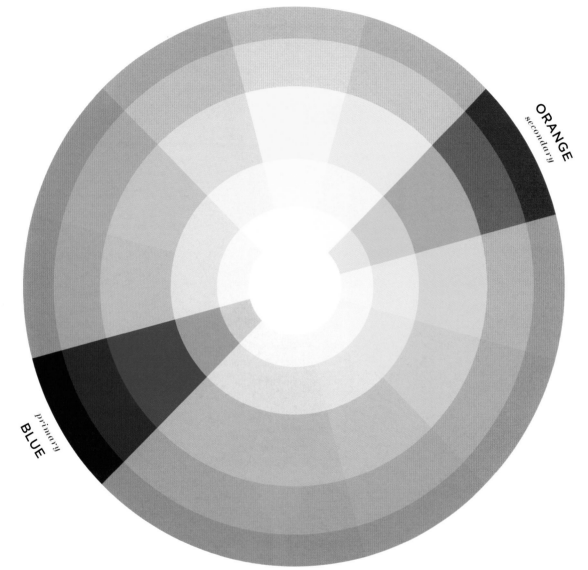

ORANGE
secondary

BLUE
primary

COMPLEMENTARY. Opposites on the
color wheel—red and green, orange
and blue, and purple and yellow—are
complementary colors. When these colors
are used together, they make each other
appear brighter and more intense. In the
kitchen *opposite* the colors are all grayed
to a degree for a richer effect.

MONOCHROMATIC. Using a single color in varying intensities is called a monochromatic color scheme. These one-color groupings are most interesting when combined with a variety of textures and patterns. This living room features a monochromatic scheme of cream, beige, and taupe, offering variety within the same color family. Keeping the drapery colors similar to the wall color creates an unbroken, enveloping backdrop, focusing the attention on the seating area.

SOOTHING PALETTE
(RIGHT) A variety of textures in the upholstery, rug, and throw adds interest to this monochromatic living room.

timeless
combinations

In the vast world of color, some hues make natural partners. Think of the crispness when blue teams with white or the warmth when red and yellow combine. Different color pairings can make a room seem peaceful or invigorating, warm or cool, large or small. Simplify the mixing process by choosing from among these enduring color schemes.

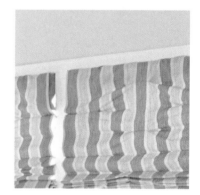

blue
& white

BELOVED HUES. Blue and white are the classics in decorating. From ticking stripes to delft tiles to French toiles, the beloved color combination has endured the decades. Often white sets the stage, and blue becomes the secondary color, creating a crisp look. This dining room, however, reverses the color scheme. Deep blue walls give the formal space a distinguished presence that complements the dark wood furnishings. Although blue is a cool color, the intensity and liberal use of it here make the room seem cozy.

WIDE RANGE. The beauty of blue is that there are so many shades from which to choose and most of them work well together. Carpet squares in light, medium, and dark shades of blue, with some creamy hues mixed in, form a custom-size rug that brightens this floor.

ACCENT COLOR (BELOW) Touches of green enliven the room. Green tends to work well with blue, since both hues are cool.

LIGHT SOURCES Dark walls are usually best served by light-color window treatments. These drapery panels, as well as the rods, rings, finials, and plantation shutters, brighten the setting.

TWO BLUES (BELOW)
Deep blue accents on the side table draw the eye in this bedroom made restful with softer blues on the walls and bed. Plenty of white bridges the blues for a clean and airy ambience.

GRAPHIC MIX (RIGHT)
This bedroom's white walls have a gallerylike quality that allows the bright blue painting to stand out.

WORTH REPEATING (LEFT) Nearly every element in this bathroom, including the trompe l'oeil plates, extends the blue-and-white theme that started with the sink.

TRADITIONAL LOOK (ABOVE) The white-painted floor and cabinets in this kitchen provide crisp contrast to the timeless toile wallpaper.

gold

GOLDEN GLOW (BELOW) Wallpaper
with shiny gold dots partners with light
brown-and-cream bedding for a cozy but
elegant look.

SOLID FOUNDATION (ABOVE) This gold-and-cream scheme is a sophisticated alternative to yellow and white. The muted tones work well in a bedroom, where relaxation is the goal.

WARMING TREND (ABOVE) Natural materials, such as bamboo, wood, and wicker, work well with gold. Hand-printed wallcovering and textured fabrics at the windows add to the warmth.

FLOWER POWER (BELOW) Bouquets and gardens can inspire pleasing color combinations. These simple yellow and red bouquets subtly echo the reddish tone of the dresser and gold walls.

DOWN UNDER
(RIGHT) Color is a factor even when selecting a natural material for floors. The light golden tone of this bamboo floor welcomes the rich contrast of the desk and chair, *above right*.

REFLECTIVE QUALITY (LEFT) Fixtures line up in a row along a black granite knee wall. The granite's polished suface lends depth to the space.

BOXED IN (BELOW) A black shadow box-style window frames the towering flower for a simple yet striking display. The terra-cotta pot brings new color and rustic texture into the sleek mix.

black & white

CONTEMPORARY CHARACTER. The bold contrast of a black-and-white plan gives a room a highly graphic look. This bathroom embraces the modern-minded personality without looking stark or allowing the black to get too dark. Natural light illuminates the rubber flooring and granite lower walls.

PERFECT PARTNERS. Silvery accents, such as shiny chrome and gleaming mirrors, are good companions in a black-and-white room, adding to the contemporary style. Don't rule out this classic combination for more traditional spaces, though, because the graphic edge can easily be toned down. Add taupe and red—along with a few timeless fabrics such as a plaid, toile, or ticking stripes—and the color scheme goes traditional.

TOTAL CONTRAST A crisp white freestanding tub creates strong contrast against the black-painted cabinetry.

decorating in
black and white

▸ A grouping of shapely vases has sculptural appeal.

▸ A wide white mat and simple black frame make a black-and-white photo more artful.

▸ Fluffy white towels, folded and stacked for presence, soften the setting.

▸ A potted white flower is a striking silhouette against the black window box.

red, white, & blue

TRADITIONAL TWIST. A red-white-and-blue scheme may bring to mind Americana style with stars and stripes, but this formal living room shows another side of the classic color grouping. Subtle stripes are brought into the mix in the upholstered chair, while the floral-and-bird motif fabric on the sofas has an exotic garden feel. The creamy linen fabric incorporates different shades of red and blue with green stepping in as an accent color.

POWER IN THREES. When you're working with a three-color palette, pay attention to balance. Here cherry red—the boldest color in the mix—is dispersed around the room so it's not overpowering. Pillows on the sofa and the painted interior of the glass-front bookcases prove that red, even when used sparingly, has big impact. For a subdued look use the lightest of your three colors for major areas, such as on walls, floors, and the largest furnishings. Although this rug is darker than the creamy white walls, it lightens the dark-stained floor and, with the walls, creates a clean canvas.

FORMAL SETTING (ABOVE) Creamy white walls relax the red accents in the living room. The bright blue of the vases on the floor draws the eye to the focal point fireplace.

COLOR CONNECTION
(RIGHT) Cherry red pillows, white flowers, and stacked books with blue covers contribute to the color palette in small ways.

white

IN FOCUS (LEFT) This mostly white setting allows the views, not the furniture, to take center stage. Drapery panels provide a soft frame.

FOCAL POINTS (ABOVE) Mesh speaker fabric on the outer doors visually softens the large custom entertainment center in the living room. Ceramics displayed in their own cubbies have impact in the white backdrop.

NEUTRAL SCENE Beige accents—the fireplace surround, plant container, and pillows—and the greenery of plants bring flashes of color into this living room.

getting it right with **white**

A white-on-white scheme can be utterly serene. Minus color, a sense of calm and order prevails.

The question is how do you keep a white room from looking cold and stark? As with most decorating plans, variety is the key. Successful white-on-white rooms are never entirely white.

As you shop for fabrics and paints, broaden your horizon by considering a pale gray or even a whisper of blue for select areas.

When you slipcover or upholster chairs and sofas in white, form becomes the most prominent feature.

Woods and metals also play a key role in a mostly white setting. Wood furniture and accents, such as drawer pulls and bowls, bring out the warm undertones in white. Metal accents, such as chrome or stainless steel, give a sleeker and visually cooler look.

MELLOW MIX (ABOVE) In the kitchen soft gray cabinets team with white—a combination that transitions easily to the stainless appliances. White tiles grouted in gray introduce a graphic pattern.

TIDY STORAGE (RIGHT) Simplicity and order are trademarks of white schemes. Kitchen staples displayed in jars provide clutter-free storage and continue the monochromatic hues.

blue
& green

ADDING ON (RIGHT)
Yellow mixes with blue
and green in this setting
to warm the cool colors.
The yellow fabrics feature
large amounts of blue for
a smooth transition.

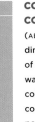

**COLORFUL
COLLECTIBLES**

(ABOVE) Delft and Spode
dinnerware add a dash
of color against green
walls. Building a room's
color plan around
collectibles gives prized
possessions prominence.

FRESH COMBINATION
Blue and green are cool and calming. In this green hall and stairwell, blue and white accessories connect the space to the adjacent room, while yellow picture mats add a lively accent.

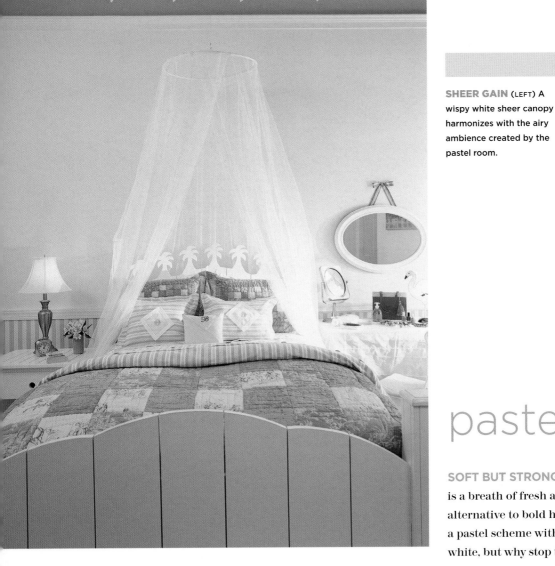

e beautiful if they are few." *Anne*

pastels

SOFT BUT STRONG. A pastel color palette is a breath of fresh air—an easy-on-the-eye alternative to bold hues. It's easy to build a pastel scheme with just one color plus white, but why stop there? The great thing about pastels is the more the merrier. In this room butter-color walls create a welcoming backdrop for pink, blue, green, and lavender.

GROWN-UP APPEAL. Although pastels are often associated with nurseries and little girls' rooms, there's a place for them in adult spaces too. Chalky tones, such as the one on the yellow footboard, work well in more sophisticated rooms. Chocolate brown or black can be striking when combined with a pastel too. When mixing these soft colors, choose ones of the same intensity—for example, colors that are all found on the same row on paint chips. This room, however, brings in bright pastels as accents for an extra splash of color.

BRIGHT SIDE (LEFT) A bubblegum-pink towel shows of the bolder side of pastels.

CLASSIC COLORS
Traditional pastels—
pinks, yellows,
and blues—are the
foundation of this room.
The breezy fabric at
the window plays to the
soft character of the
color scheme.

red &
yellow

GREEN DIVERSION (BELOW) In a room of red and yellow, the muted green sofa and ottoman work with other green accents to provide resting places for the eye.

warming up with **red and yellow**

Red is dramatic wherever it's used, and when it's paired with yellow a room really heats up.

Because both are warm colors, a red-and-yellow scheme can take the chill out of a cold space, such as a northern-exposure living room. Conversely, this classic pairing has so much visual warmth that it may be too much for a sunroom.

When working with red and yellow consider your goal. If you want a very cozy room, use the two colors liberally. Red or yellow walls, patterned upholstered furnishings, and accessories that repeat the two colors will provide warmth. If you want something that's still warm but not quite so cozy, keep walls neutral and cool things down with touches of green or blue.

VISUAL ANCHOR

(ABOVE) Solid-color red sofas dominate this family room, where the creamy yellow bookcase becomes a neutralizer.

PATTERN MIX (LEFT) Similar to the way an accent color stands out in a setting, the exotic pattern of this yellow pillow makes a statement against the florals.

ADDING INTEREST (RIGHT) Embroidered details and lacy sheers ensure that the cream scheme has visual appeal.

cream & pink

QUIET TIME. When the look you're after is soft and sweet, there's no better combination than cream and pink. The romantic scheme is a hallmark of cottage-style decorating, yet it's versatile enough to slip into traditional settings. The key is to choose mellow tones. In this living room cream, rather than stark white, and pale pink, rather than bubblegum, provide a tranquil quality.

SURROUND YOURSELF. To balance a cream-and-pink scheme—or any palette for that matter—let one color dominate. Cream takes the lead in this room, where the ottoman becomes a canvas for a sprinkling of pink accessories. The pink flowers and the floral pattern on the tea set gain visual impact in the colorless setting. Though grand in size, the ottoman doesn't command too much attention, thanks to cream-color fabric.

DASHING DETAILS (ABOVE) Plush peonies, a tea set, and a glass chandelier blend into the serene space.

blue & yellow

SUNNY OUTLOOK. A blue-and-yellow scheme is a favorite for a reason: It's a happy combination. The two primary colors play off each other in this office/guest suite. Mustard-yellow walls warm the space, and blue fabrics and accessories cool things down. The lively palette incorporates light and dark shades of both hues—from indigo to powder, saffron to butter. White furnishings and trim keep the look bright.

WIDESPREAD APPEAL. A blue-and-yellow palette is a popular choice for his-and-hers spaces, incorporating colors that appeal to both genders. Although the color scheme is often associated with country French style, this office/guest suite has a more playful quality. Polka dots on the lampshade, rug, and fabric skirt are a lighthearted contrast to the traditional toiles and damask used for some of the pillows on the daybed.

COLOR SHIFT (ABOVE) Bright blue knobs accentuate drawers painted in graduating intensities of yellow. Closet doors on the opposite wall feature yellow knobs, *opposite above*.

details make the difference

Pillows incorporate the fresh color scheme in different ways.

The shades' fabric ribbons and blue backing coordinate with the pillows.

Red tulips pull in the third primary color, making the yellow and blue pop.

Textured plaster gives the yellow walls the look of suede.

earthtones

SUPPORTING CAST (BELOW) The lighter hues of the sea-grass cube-style ottoman and the earthy rug and ceiling fan allow the brown leather club chairs to star.

REST EASY (LEFT) Even a monochromatic scheme needs a visual resting place. Here the solid taupe tablecloth repeats the wood tint on the chairs and provides respite.

easy color

A palette of browns, taupes, beiges, and creams is easy on the eye and soothing to the spirit.

MONOCHROMATIC MAGIC. The rooms featured here illustrate the most common monochromatic palette of browns, taupes, beiges, and creams. These earthy combinations need never be bland, as tonal variations can create subtle differences that are ideal when you want serenity.

TEXTURAL INTRIGUE. When building a room with earthy neutrals, you're forced to think beyond color. Diverse texture is key. Wicker, rattan, and bamboo lend warmth and dimension, as do nubby fabrics and rugs. Smooth finishes, such as coppers and bronzes, can also be worked in. They provide a more formal look compared to casual wicker and rattan.

LAYERS OF DEPTH

(RIGHT) A mix of textures, including a grass-cloth wall covering and woven bombé chest, gives a tan-and-cream scheme dimension and depth.

LIGHT TOUCH (ABOVE) The neutral palette of this light-filled living room provides a hidden bonus. Minus color, there's minimal worry about fabrics fading from all the sunlight.

LAYERED LOOK

(RIGHT) This bed gains interest from layering rather than from color. Pillows draw the eye to the headboard—a carved screen that anchors the setting and lends striking contrast to the earthtones.

REFINED MIX (BELOW) Smooth textures give a neutral scheme a formal look. This room's brassy mirror and candelabras are focal points, offering contrast to the casual nubby rug.

PERFECT PARTNERS (BELOW) A mix of traditional and contemporary wicker pieces provides a tropical flourish and proves that matched sets aren't a requirement for style.

red & white

MODERN THINKING (RIGHT)
A red-and-white scheme is highly adaptable, working in traditional, country, or modern settings. With a leather chair and faux fur rug, the look here is contemporary.

LIGHT LOOK (BELOW)
White is an instant brightener; it punches up any color it's paired with. On these shades red banding accentuates the color contrast.

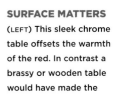

SURFACE MATTERS
(LEFT) This sleek chrome table offsets the warmth of the red. In contrast a brassy or wooden table would have made the reds seem even warmer.

FOCUS HERE
A pair of red sofas,
outlined with crisp
white piping, serves as
a dramatic focal point
for this seating area.

style

No matter what style you love, there is a color palette you can bring in to enhance the look and make it completely yours. The rooms that follow show you only some of the beautiful color options that complement a variety of styles.

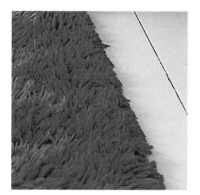

LOOK HERE To focus attention on one key piece, this Chippendale sofa was re-covered in a large-patterned French cotton print that stands out amid the soft blues of the other large-scale patterns.

traditional

MANY MOODS. Just as there are many ways to accessorize and personalize a simple, elegant black dress, you'll discover nearly unlimited approaches to traditional style. It can be formal and sophisticated, casual, or even unexpectedly whimsical—the decision is yours. Although the furnishings and accessories play the primary role in establishing style, color can serve as the frosting on the cake and the element that influences ambience. Use rich hues mixed with dark woods, for example, for a moody library look. Or consider a pale monochromatic palette for an airy, serene setting. Even dark-wood, classic furniture can be transformed into surprisingly lighthearted fare if you paint it or experiment with playful pattern and colors for the upholstery, pillows, walls, and rug. If you'd like to mix patterns, as was done so successfully in the room shown here, select fabrics that share a common color.

REFRESHED CLASSIC This living room blows the dust off tradition and takes on a lively look with bold, yet classic, graphics done in vibrant hues of blue with punches of red.

FOREVER COZY (ABOVE) The mellow golden tones of the wood wall paneling make this living room a warm and inviting retreat.

SHINED UP (ABOVE) The charcoal-color walls in this dining room are made subtly reflective with a sheen of wax. A variety of whites gives the room added dimension.

SCREEN STARS (LEFT) Tall green freestanding screens, which feature traditional recessed-panel styling, pull color all the way to the ceiling of this white-walled living room. Green-and-cream pillows draw the color onto the sofa.

BASIC BLACK (BELOW) There's something about black that instantly adds elegance to a room, and this kitchen is no exception. Paired with yellow-painted walls and tongue-and-groove siding, the dark hue stands out without making the space oppressive.

CLEAN BREAK (ABOVE)
You don't need a lot of color to make a big style statement. In this dining room pristine shades of white create an airy balance with the golden hues of the pine table and wide floor planks.

HAPPILY SINGLE (BELOW)
For unpretentious country sophistication, use a single color with a "dirty neutral" backdrop. In this dining room the painted blue hutch, chairs, table, and collections make a dramatic impact.

country

WELCOME HOME. Although country style can be dressed up for a refined look or toned down to be farmhouse casual, it always feels relaxed and inviting. Think of it as a style that romances the ordinary—vintage sign letters stand in as artwork or a wooden toolbox becomes a humble yet handsome container for a profusion of flowers. If you like a more rustic, primitive feel, complement country-style elements with a palette of muted tones, such as the blue-splashed dining room *opposite*. Or give country a refreshing update with more vibrant hues, such as the apple green and cherry red used in the bedroom *right*. You may want to live more simply and layer your home in shades of white mixed with the warmth of wood, such as in the dining room *above*.

FOREVER SPRING (ABOVE)

A cabin-style bedroom bursts out of the woods with lively spring green window treatments paired with a bright red-and-white check comforter.

PARIS CHIC (ABOVE) An early 1800s dressy French parlor couch, upholstered in a rich chocolate-brown velvet with taupe brush fringe, displays a collection of plush pillows—some with the look of old tapestries. The floor-to-ceiling gilded mirror leans against a deep caramel-color wall for a look of casual elegance.

GOOD NIGHT (BELOW) A neutral color scheme makes for restful surroundings in this bedroom, which features an 18th-century French bed as the centerpiece. The oversize bedside table has a worn painted finish for a vintage look.

french

STYLE STARTERS. Classic blue and yellow or palettes of earthtones all harmonize with French furnishings.

To create French style mix and match those hues and bring in four elements: scale, warmth, wit, and pattern.

Experiment with large-scale pieces. Select an armoire; an overscale mirror, such as the one *opposite*; or a bulky table.

Introduce warmth with color, textures, and layers. One classic French approach is to arrange flowers or plants in an urn. Or layer three skirts, such as on this bed *left*. The living room *opposite* mixes velvet and wicker.

Add whimsy to a room. The zebra rug in the living room *opposite* is an unexpected touch.

Vary patterns. In the family room *above*, two floral designs keep the look refreshing and interesting.

FRUIT FLAVOR (LEFT) A stainless-steel bowl filled with one kind of fruit lends zip to a minimalist setting.

ACCENT ON BLACK (LEFT) Blocks of black and white distinguish this contemporary cabinet.

contemporary

MODERN MUSINGS. Think of the shortest route on a map, and you begin to understand the heart of contemporary style: The route can be curving, straight, or a bit of both, but you want to get to your destination with minimal fuss. That's contemporary style—a look that honors clean lines, smooth or sleek surfaces, and sculptural ingenuity.

This kitchen is a striking example of how curves and crisp geometrics can beautifully coexist. And although there is an abundance of chrome, silver, and white, the space isn't cold thanks to the generous doses of warm woods and cheery punches of yellow.

Black is always welcome in a contemporary space, lending elegance and definition to artwork, architecture, and special features. In this kitchen black leads the eye throughout the room from the staircase to the stepped cabinet to the island countertop and console beyond.

Feel free to use any color palette that suits you. In a contemporary space you can have fun with a rainbow of colors or only one or two.

WARM WOODS Using the eye-pleasing tones of wood in a contemporary space ensures a welcoming look. In this loft kitchen/gathering room, visual warmth radiates from the bamboo flooring.

SILK SENSATIONS (ABOVE) Asian themes lend themselves well to the use of colorful silk fabrics. This bedroom sitting area features window panels of contrasting silk and cotton squares.

FURNISHED FLAIR

(LEFT) A pair of side-by-side Chinese wedding chests anchors one wall of the bedroom and sets the pace for the colors selected for the walls and carpeting. The bamboo bed frame repeats the tones of the chests for a serene look.

VISUAL OOMPH (LEFT)
Restful golden hues are made
more interesting with the
textural beauty of the subtle
square-motif bedspread and
the bamboo bed as well as
the dramatic black bombé
chest and black-and-white
check pillows.

asian

FARAWAY FLAVOR. Valued for its worldly
flair and sophistication, Asian style is also
prized for the air of calm it exudes. Use
a number of strategies to complement
Asian furnishings and accessories.

Consider painting and glazing walls to
create a soft, ethereal backdrop. In this
bedroom, for example, glaze over paint
lends a cloudy effect.

Use a monochromatic palette. Painting
walls, trim, and the ceiling in similar
mellow hues enhances the sense of
serenity. Choosing furnishings in the
same warm tones keeps the look seamless.

Introduce texture. Bamboo, rattan,
wicker, and sisal are just a few examples
of textural pieces you can use to promote
Asian style. Painting techniques also can
add texture; here, the glaze over paint
is applied in a crosshatch pattern that
resembles linen.

Enliven with accent colors. Black and
red are two bold colors that can punch
up an Asian color scheme and give it
distinction and interest.

COLOR FIESTA (RIGHT) The punchy chartreuse paint on these cabinets was inspired by the decor of a Mexican hotel favored by the homeowners.

spanish

LIVELY OR LAID-BACK. As the popularity of Spanish style grows, manufacturers are taking the guesswork out of selecting a suitable palette. Look for coordinated color schemes ready-made for you in the paint aisle.

If you want to create a festive atmosphere, consider bright hues. For inspiration turn to items that already feature Latin flair, such as indigenous dishware or fabrics. This kitchen *above right* and *opposite above* kicks up its heels with chartreuse green on the cabinets and bold red, yellow, blue, and green striped fabric on the banquette cushions. Shaker-style cabinets feature full-size doors that don't reveal the cabinet box, providing an uncluttered canvas for the paint. Too much detail would compete with the color.

For a less prominent palette use the hues from your inspiration piece but select slightly less saturated or muted versions of the same color. The color schemes for the dining and family rooms *right* and *opposite below* were developed using this technique.

DESERT HUES (BELOW) Muted reds and mustards—toned-down versions of colors found in the homeowners' art collection—complement this Spanish Colonial home. A spectacular red-and-green Bessarabian rug sets the tone in the dining room.

PATTERN PLAYS (BELOW) In the family room Spanish-inspired colors become more prominent in the patterns of the upholstered pieces.

STRIPED CELEBRATION (ABOVE) Multicolor cushions on the banquette give the room a tropical feel. Dark stain on the fir flooring helps balance the strong color.

swedish

LOW-KEY LIVING. If you want to create an airy and restful retreat, look to the influence of classic Swedish country style. Known for its pared-down, unfussy attitude, this style usually begins with pale, harmonious color—creams, warm whites, and soft blues or greens. White- or cream-painted furnishings are typically paired with the golden hues of rustic pine furnishings and pale wood flooring. Pickled or whitewashed woods also work well with the look. Stick with simple fabric patterns, such as checks and petite florals. Delicate lace, used with restraint, also enhances the effect.

ARTFUL ARCHES
Architecture plays out the Swedish theme with highly stylized acanthus-leaf motifs painted in pale aqua.

HANDPAINTED DETAIL This subtle, naturalistic handpainted element on the wall above the pine desk is typical of Swedish country houses in the 18th and 19th centuries.

old world

AGED PERFECTION. Bring the relaxed
beauty of a Mediterranean farmhouse to
your home. To re-create an old-world
atmosphere, strive for finishes, colors,
and materials that appear rustic,
weathered, and well-worn. Faded and
muted colors for this style reflect the
sunny climate of the region.

Introduce shades of nature in stone
floors and countertops and the warm
tones of wood. Distressing new surfaces,
such as wood cabinets, can prevent them
from appearing out of place in an aged
setting. Black stain, rubbed on and then
rubbed off wood surfaces, settles into
dents and grooves obscuring the newness
of the material.

Walls can be similarly "weathered" using
roughed plaster painted in light, sunny
hues. Darker glazes, rubbed on and wiped
off the plaster, instantly ages walls.

HISTORY UNDERFOOT
(ABOVE) Tumbled marble
floor tiles appear as though
they were rescued from an
ancient building and reused
in the kitchen.

AGED ILLUSIONS Custom-made knotty pine cabinets are lightly stained and waxed to allow the natural hues of the wood to warm the kitchen. The edges of the orange marble countertop have been distressed for an antique feel.

FADED GLORY (LEFT)
A prize Napoleon III chair upholstered in faded period paisley feels fresh and playful when paired with the white-painted Moroccan table.

cottage

OUTDOOR INSPIRATION. Like a garden, cottage style can be eye-popping and vibrant with color, or cool and subtle as a spring breeze. The palette you pick depends on the mood you want to create, but the furnishings and accessories should always be, or appear to be, vintage or antique. Garden-related items and floral motifs will also enhance your cottage-style room.

If you prefer to feel invigorated when you walk into a room, go for the bold, such as the lively attitude offered by the bright red walls in the living room *opposite*. To balance the vibrancy of the walls and to ensure that the space doesn't appear contemporary, the door and floor are soft Depression-era green.

FLOWER FINESSE
(LEFT) Roses inspire colors and motifs that are quintessentially cottage style, such as floral pattern fabrics.

BOLD MOVE Deep red walls initiate the warm backdrop for this cottage-style room. Pairing the deep color with pale green for the door and floor adds garden flair.

SUBTLE STRIPES

(RIGHT) Two tones of sea green paint form wide stripes on these bedroom walls. The colors set off the white-painted furniture and make the pink floral-and-ticking stripe fabrics on the chair a focal point.

NEW TO OLD (LEFT) New unfinished chairs such as these can suit a cottage-style theme when instantly aged. Use a paintbrush to apply white latex paint that's thinned with water to the consistency of light cream. When dry, sand some spots to appear worn.

AIRY ADDITIONS (LEFT)
Furniture dressed in white is
always welcome. This sink-in
soft goose-down sofa features
a crisp white slipcover teamed
with a white-painted garden
bench and a pair of distressed-
picket side tables.

DINING DE-LIGHT Pale greens
and blues echo the French tin sign
on the wall, making this dining room
a breezy cottage-garden delight.
Tailored slipcovers that button up the
back prevent the pastel hues from
appearing too feminine.

FLYING FOCUS (ABOVE)
This Mobil Pegasus sign
without question sets the
pace for the living room.
Sofas upholstered in yellow,
pink, and red enhance the
playful mood.

SHAG RETURNS (RIGHT) A brilliant orange shag rug teams with a shapely pair of chrome-legged lounge chairs to inject the space with retro flavor.

retro

BACK TO THE FUTURE. Call it modern or mid-century, retro styles and colors from the '40s, '50s, and '60s are hip. The look is active, energizing, and a bit nostalgic, putting the focus on fun, as in the sitting area *above* and in the living room *opposite*. The look can also be elegantly simple, however, such as in the dining room right, where subtle hues and clean lines yield a quieter setting. Check out today's color trends beginning on page 90 to discover many color palettes that complement retro style—bright orange and apple green, aqua and chocolate brown, and bold red and hot pink are only some of the more fashion-forward choices. In a toned-down modern setting, try silvers and champagnes spiked with bursts of red and yellow to set off mid-century furnishings.

SMOOTH LANDING (BELOW) Stackable chairs and Swiss Air memorabilia establish this dining room's sense of mid-century modern design. Tropical flowers provide bursts of bright color without interrupting the quiet elegance of the space.

trends

Like fashion, color goes in cycles—getting a new name and new interpretation with each return performance. Yesterday's rust is today's spicy paprika. If you like to live on the cutting edge, these are some of the combinations you'll see in home furnishings, fabrics, paint, and accessories.

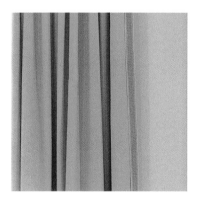

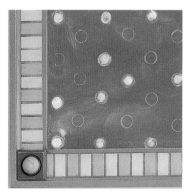

BRUSH STROKES (ABOVE)
Paint isn't only for walls. In this room pink and green paints extend the colors to the dotted lampshade, artwork, and a wooden "N."

pink
& green

THINK PINK. Pink is the comeback color of recent years. Fashionable in the '50s—and always beloved in little girls' bedrooms—pink has made its way back into adult decorating schemes. When the hue veers to the bright side and teams with apple green—as it does in this living room—the look is fresh and fun. At once playful and classic, it's a color combination that brings cheer to the dreariest room.

BRIGHTEN WITH WHITE. If you crave a hot-pink and apple-green room but are afraid of overdoing it, stick with white walls. White creates a simple, clean canvas for showing off colorful furnishings and accessories. Keep in mind that white comes in a wide range of shades, from yellowish creams to bluish whites; in this room a bright white paint with a pink undertone was the perfect choice.

CURTAIN TIME (ABOVE)
Curtains shouldn't be strictly
utilitarian. These draperies
of delicate silver, gold, and
gray fabric glisten when
light falls across them.

metallics

For the ultimate in elegance bring a
little sheen into your decorating scheme
with metallics that bring to mind luxury
and richness.

Today's designs move beyond
traditional silver and gold. Consider
pewter and champagne for a gentler
and modern-minded version that still
embodies elegance. And be prepared to
shift your thinking on what a metallic
is: Fabrics and paints can add as much
shimmer as mirrors, furnishings,
and accessories.

Subtlety is the key to a soothing pewter-
and-champagne scheme. The palette can
encompass quiet color, such as pale grays,
pinkish creams, muted bronzes, and soft
golds. Surfaces should shimmer but not
shine so brightly that they're jarring.
Consider silky fabrics, hazy old mirrors,
and butter-soft leathers. Choose light
fixtures that bathe the room in a soft
glow. Chandeliers, low-wattage lamps, and
even candles will show off pewter and
champagne best, bouncing and dancing
the light across the room.

SCREEN GEM (LEFT)
Nailhead trim on this creamy
leather screen provides an
elegant backdrop for the
more burnished tone of the
scrolled table.

pink & turquoise

CULTURAL FUSION. A wide world of color awaits any room—literally. Some of the most interesting color schemes take inspiration from cultures that celebrate color. Think of the tropical hues of the Caribbean, the rich jewel tones of India, or the primary-splashed geometrics of West Africa. This home celebrates the saturated colors of Mexico, with deep pink walls and turquoise kitchen cabinetry.

UNLIKELY PARTNERS. Some color combinations push the boundaries of logic and can even be startling—and that's the fun. The pink and turquoise scheme in this kitchen is an example: things get even more curious in the dining room, where the pink walls transition to an orange study. Similar to the trend in mismatched furnishings, clashing colors have gained acceptance. When choosing colors keep in mind that experimenting with color combinations can yield beautiful results.

INSPIRATION POINTS (ABOVE & RIGHT) Let fresh vegetables, fruits, and flowers provide ideas for unique color pairings. Choose colors of the same intensity for the best results.

gold

GOLD MINE (RIGHT) No longer a throwback to the '70s, gold and orange have thoroughly modern appeal, especially when set against creamy white for crispness. Green is a natural accent color; the large art piece calms the sizzling color combo.

JUICY HUE (BELOW) Vibrant cantaloupe-colored draperies and a lively area rug bring a sunny glow to a room that doesn't get direct sunlight. An orange-and-yellow palette is ideal for northern exposure rooms.

MIXED UP (LEFT) The mix-and-match trend is evident in these dining chairs that alternate cream upholstery with a cheerful yellow pattern. A bowl of fruit plays to the color scheme.

VARIETY PACK (ABOVE) Accessories are a great way to experiment with color because they don't require long-term commitment. These pillows share a similarity in color—gold and orange are connected by yellow—while the mix of wide-weave cottons and stylized prints adds textural variety.

EYE CATCHER (RIGHT) A fun fabric can have as much impact as artwork. These pillows, in fact, take the place of art; walls are simply covered with mirrors to allow the fabric to shine.

ICEBREAKER (ABOVE) Blue is a cool hue, and when the tint is steely, as in this bedroom, it especially benefits from a warm partner. Touches of brown—most notably the velvet bedcover—cozy up with the icy blue.

brown
& blue

BROWN BRIGADE. Brown is the new neutral that works with all colors and in any room. Although the hue is abundant in nature, brown does not condemn your rooms to dirt-bland style. The varying tones of brown—such as chocolate, mocha, and toffee—can launch a delicious color scheme.

BLUE STREAK. The pairing of blue and brown is fast becoming a classic. Explore the vast range of blues, from turquoise and sky blue to Wedgwood blue and sapphire. Browns can certainly be incorporated into a room with paint and fabrics, but keep in mind that stained wood furnishings and cabinetry also contribute rich color and important contrast to any shade of blue.

COOL HARMONY
Combining pale purple with white trim and furnishings creates a serene environment, perfect for relaxing after a long day.

LAYERED LUXURY
(LEFT) Shimmering fabrics and glowing walls show the opulent side of purple in this bedroom. White linens and accessories make the deep hue even more lush and dramatic.

purple

Associated with royalty—and sometimes mystery—purple comes in a breadth of tones and conjures many images.

A lavender scheme with lots of white worked in can be spring-fresh and cottagelike, while an amethyst-and-gold theme can be opulent. When a mix of purples is worked into one room, there's an instant wow factor. The key to making sure an all-purple room doesn't become cartoonish is to combine a wide range of tones—lavender, deep raspberry, plum, and eggplant—and textures. Think velvets, silks, crystals, and suedes when the goal is a room that is ultra-glamorous.

When designing with one or two colors—be it purple, pink, or green—choose a focal point because a monochromatic scheme can easily become boring. Your focal point could be a window seat, a floor screen, a piece of artwork—such as in the pale purple bedroom *opposite*—or even elegant bedding, such as in the bedroom *left*. Variety is key even when limiting the design to one color family.

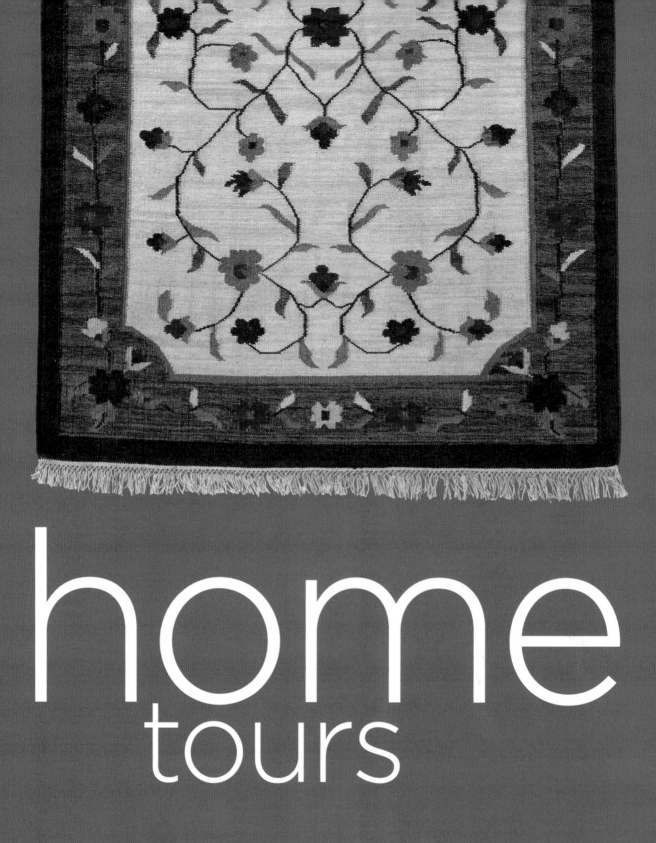

home
tours

Used in a conscientious manner, color is the glue that holds your home's decorating scheme together. Whether you prefer warm, vibrant colors; cool, serene colors; or a combination of the two, there is a whole-house color scheme that will work for you.

cohesive color

COLOR SUCCESS. Color is the strongest visual connector for making the rooms in your home appear well planned. You can achieve a cohesive look by flowing your chosen color palette from room to room, creating a seamless appearance.

TINT TRICKS. The owner of this Connecticut home wanted different colors everywhere—on the walls, rugs, furnishings, accessories, and artwork. To make such a diverse palette work, she enlisted the help of Iliana Moore of Columbine Antiques and Decorations.

At Moore's suggestion, the interior paint colors were all lightened with the same amount of white (as shown on the color wheel on page 25), making them compatible to the eye. "Picking colors of a similar tint makes most any color combination work," Moore says. Her other color trick? "I like to accessorize connecting rooms with accent pieces that match the wall color in the adjacent room," she says. "It's a simple color trick that makes the overall design scheme appear more cohesive."

SPRING FEVER (RIGHT)
The home's entryway is painted a fresh, clean light green—the color of early spring. A white-painted archway separates the entry from the peach-color dining room. Using white woodwork throughout the home unifies the appearance of each room.

WARM AMBIENCE The coral color of the dining room walls is both appetizing and energizing. New green frames on the bird prints create a color connection between this room and the entryway shown on the previous page.

COOL ATTITUDE (ABOVE)
Like the sky on a summer day, pastel blues make the gathering room feel peaceful and serene, underscoring its role as the perfect place to relax after entertaining in the dining room or to steal away and enjoy a good book.

WARMTH AND RELAXATION
(LEFT) Part of the living room, this area was set up to accommodate reading. The soft colors encourage relaxation, while the red chairs offer contrast.

FLORAL FANCY The two-tone floral fabric used on the window treatments and sofa was the inspiration for the bedroom's color combination.

FRESH MIX A contrast of warm browns and cool blues creates an enticing ambience.

color and **mood**

Draw an imaginary vertical line down the middle of the color wheel.

On the left are the cool colors—watery blues, restful greens, and dreamy violets. These colors make a room feel cooler and more serene.

The right side of the color wheel is filled with warm, active colors—sunny yellows, stimulating oranges, and energizing reds. These colors make a room feel warmer and more vibrant.

This home features an alluring combination of each—warm, vibrant colors are used in the kitchen and dining area. Cool, calm colors adorn the living room and bedrooms. "Our goal was to make each room's function and mood compatible while working together throughout the house," Iliana Moore says.

POWER PLAY (LEFT) The kitchen opens to the family room but is separated from the rest of the house by a long hall. Because of this Moore felt comfortable using stronger colors in these two rooms. The wall color matches one of the backsplash tiles. Its intensity makes the large room cozier.

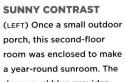

SUNNY CONTRAST (LEFT) Once a small outdoor porch, this second-floor room was enclosed to make a year-round sunroom. The deep royal blue provides cool contrast against the warm sunshine.

HERE AND THERE
The yellow wall color extends into the family gathering area and sets off the stucco fireplace.

SPARE CHANGE (ABOVE) Less is more in the dining room, where accents are simple and spare. The dark-stained round alderwood table was custom-made to have an aged and distressed appearance while the lacquered finish brings durability. A large mirror gives visual depth to the narrow room.

total contrast

OPPOSITES ATTRACT. The simple black-and-white color scheme used throughout this California home suggests a casual lifestyle and eclectic tastes. Following the style is easy: All the walls in the two-story townhouse are painted warm white. Wood furnishings in each room are, for the most part, black or blackish-brown. Upholstery is white. Windows are left bare to allow in more sunlight.

Accessories bring additional pattern and texture to the design and, on occasion, dollops of color. Artwork is homegrown: Black-and-white prints made from family photos are mounted in similar frames.

UNIFYING COLOR. The color principle couldn't be simpler—color unifies styles. Designer Paula Stein describes the mix of furnishings in this townhome as "Zen beach cottage." The mix consists of simple Asian-inspired elements such as a contemporary four-poster and round mirrors as well as classic beach-cottage elements including beaded board, wood floors, and wainscoting.

FRESH FACE (ABOVE) Sunshine yellow flowers and decorative accessories keep the table decor fresh and interesting.

SIMPLE PLEASURE (BELOW) A round mirror and candlesticks make the fireplace mantel a focal point while underscoring the simplicity of the design scheme.

LIGHT ILLUSIONS The pale palette of the living room reflects light, making the room appear more spacious. Mocha- and black-striped toss pillows were chosen to meld with the stain color used on the wood floors.

FLOWER POWER (ABOVE) Boldly patterned toss pillows punch up the daybed in the guest bedroom. A green floor basket adds a spot of unexpected color.

COTTAGE CONNECTION (RIGHT) In the guest bath, bright white beaded-board wainscoting subtly contrasts with the warm white walls. Artwork and mirror are all framed in black.

UNDER COVER (ABOVE) Throughout the home's private areas, a pale sand color floor covering warms the black-and-white palette and disguises beach sand and pet hair. Window treatments in the office were a concession to control glare on the computer screen.

GRAPHIC DESIGN
A creamy-white-painted-
drywall fireplace mantel
simplifies an awkward
corner of the master
bedroom. As in the dining
room, the mantel display
is simple and graphic.

NEAT NICHE (ABOVE) A black four-poster makes a strong design statement. Military-style bedding underscores the room's orderly appearance.

PILLOW POINT (RIGHT) Black monograms and a striped border add contrast to the otherwise white linens. A black photographic accent pillow adds a touch of artistry.

ASSURANCE
(ABOVE) Originally
stained dark brown,
the dining set was
updated with warm
coral paint.

REVELATION (BELOW) This painting,
along with the coral-painted table and
chairs in the dining room, set the palette
for designer Suzanne Radi.

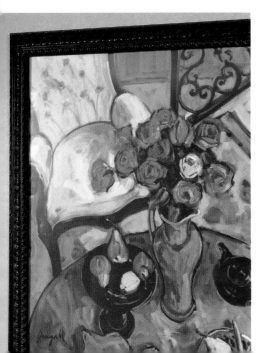

tonal tactics

INSPIRATION POINT. The painting
below left was the springboard for the
first floor color palette used in this
suburban Chicago home. Interior
designer Suzanne Radi says the
homeowners love color but lacked the
confidence to pursue it.

When one of them shared with Radi
that the room featured in the painting
looks like one she'd love to create,
Radi instantly knew they would be
comfortable drenching the home in
vibrant mood-brightening hues.

TINTS AND TONES. Like many
designers Radi doesn't commit to any
specific color formula. She does, however.
pay attention to the tonality of color,
choosing hues that are tinted with the
same amount of white or toned with
the same amount of black. "By using
similar color values, you can make any
combination work," Radi says.

TONALITY Originally painted lemon yellow, the wall color in the living room is toned down to a darker honey mustard. "Adding the brown tones to the walls worked to complement some of the wood pieces in the room and the bamboo shades," Radi says. "It also made the intensity of the colors in the chairs and the walls more similar."

CHIC LOOK (ABOVE) The dining room decor was nearly complete when Radi came on the scene. "This room really illustrates a love of color and a chic sense of style," Radi says. "The only change we made was to deepen the blue of the walls a bit to keep the tonality consistent."

UNIFYING THREADS
(RIGHT) This rug was purchased after the interior was painted. "It ties all the wall colors you can see in the adjoining spaces together," Radi says.

PLAYFUL PALETTE
(ABOVE) "You only have one chance to make a good first impression," says Radi. "In this house, the moment you step inside you feel a sense of lightheartedness and of this being a happy home."

PERSONALITY PLUS (BELOW)
"Pulling the wall color of the foyer into the living room serves as a visual invitation to come in," Radi says.

To make a whole-house color scheme cohesive, the dominant color in one room should become a supporting player in the adjacent space. For example, the blue trim of the living room window treatment and the colors in the toss pillows all relate to the colors in the dining room. The wall color used in the foyer adorns the back of the bookcases in the living room. The dining chair cushions pull in colors from the living room. "Transitions are the key to pulling everything together," Radi says.

She cautions that when using bright colors, be wary of overstimulating the senses. "More isn't always better," Radi continues. "Mixing brights with neutrals brings a sense of balance to a color scheme." For this reason Radi opted to leave the living room floor color neutral, keeping the focus on the furnishings and artwork.

COLOR EMPHASIS
(LEFT) Color extends to
the exterior where deep
blue siding gives the
suburban home the
look of an upscale
cottage. Dark
pumpernickel-color
window casings draw
attention to the home's
architectural details. As
in the front, a red door
makes the entrance a
focal point.

CURB APPEAL (LEFT)
Front porch furnishings
are adorned with the
same cheerful color
palette as the interiors.

MUTUAL INTEREST (LEFT)
The family room is painted the same color as the kitchen. A cream color fabric used on the chairs balances the muddy hues of the walls and the rug. All of the trim and bookcases have a natural finish, giving the area more of a rustic feel.

COMMON THREAD (BELOW)
The green used on the kitchen walls is also found in the living room oil painting, on the chair cushions in the dining room, and in the rug in the foyer.

ADULT DEPARTURE

The master bedroom serves as a respite from the vibrant color scheme used throughout the rest of the house. "With so much color everywhere else, we opted to make the bedroom a calm retreat. The walls are painted a warm white and the attitude is one of tranquillity," Radi says.

LIVELY SURROUND (RIGHT) Equipped with four different color chairs, this attic office accommodates homework for all four family members. The dormers are painted a bright green and the longest wall is painted blue.

color and **light**

When choosing colors for your home, it is important to look at paint and fabric samples in the area of the room where they will be applied to see how they look throughout the day. A pale green rug that looks great in the morning light may seem washed out under the afternoon sun.

To ensure the colors chosen for this home interior were exactly right, the owners looked at color chips for several days in a row and analyzed how the colors looked in varying degrees of daylight. In addition interior designer Suzanne Radi had recessed lights installed in the living room and dining room ceilings. "The key to making a space look warm and inviting anytime of day is to light it properly," Radi says.

MIXED MATCH (LEFT) Matching frames and mats give a mixed collection of prints a more cohesive appearance. The prints served as the inspiration for the loft's overall color scheme.

art start

NEW BEGINNING. Abstract paintings were the inspiration for the color scheme used in this Minneapolis loft. The turquoise, maize, red, tangerine, and lime all sprang from the art collection at left.

In each room the colors appear in a different place, proportion, and pattern, which leads the eye from room to room. For example blue appears as flowers on the duvet in the bedroom, as a cushion stripe in the dressing room, and as a blue velvet chair and a square on the sofa pillows in the living room. In the dining room art and vases bear blue. Similarly doses of tangerine and lime can be seen in varying degrees throughout the loft.

"Color used in different ways and different proportions keep the space feeling alive and large," says interior designer Tom Gunkelman, who designed the space with Lucy Searls and Karen Kinsella.

WALL TINT. The quartz fireplace surround in the living room inspired the wall colors used throughout the loft. In a completely different take on color, four gradients of warm taupe are applied to the walls following this plan: Use the lightest tint on the major walls to amplify sunlight. Use the darkest tone to draw attention to art walls and niches, the fireplace, and special antiques. Use the two midtones on walls of secondary emphasis.

KITCHEN CONNECTION (BELOW) Looking at the sofa from this angle reveals patchwork toss pillows that create a visual connection to the cattail-color stain used on the kitchen cabinets.

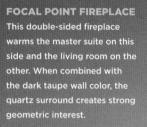

FOCAL POINT FIREPLACE
This double-sided fireplace
warms the master suite on this
side and the living room on the
other. When combined with
the dark taupe wall color, the
quartz surround creates strong
geometric interest.

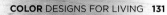

DOLLOPS OF COLOR
Unexpected accents of red-
orange make the bed a focal
point of the master suite.
Varying patterns and sizes
ensure a comfortable mix.

STANDOUT COLOR The blue chair and the orange artwork, with colors that are opposites on the color wheel, serve as the focus of this area, while the suedelike sofa in the foreground blends in with the floor covering.

Nature's colors appear throughout the space by way of fresh flowers and potted plants. "Potted plants and flowers bring a sense life to a room, so I use them whenever I can," Searls explains.

For a consistent look the design team chose brushed nickel for door and cabinet hardware and faucets because its matte-luster appearance bridges the classic-contemporary gap.

While everything else mixes, nothing matches, and that's exactly what the designers intended. "Mix something light with something dark, something woven with something plush," Kinsella says. "Rooms are more interesting that way."

MEDIA MIX (BELOW) Colorful paintings dress most walls in this loft, but a charcoal drawing and a black-and-white photo star in the den. Why the switch? "Black-and-white art offers a crisp look without overpowering the vibrant colors of the furnishings," Tom Gunkelman explains.

rooms

Magnify your kitchen's sense of coziness. Brighten the mood of the guest bath. Encourage a sense of relaxation each time you step into the master bedroom. By choosing the right color palette, you can enhance your interiors, making them as comforting and inviting as possible.

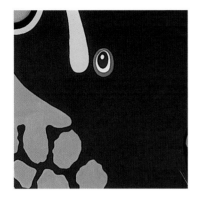

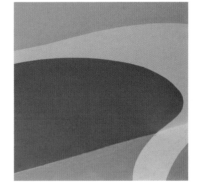
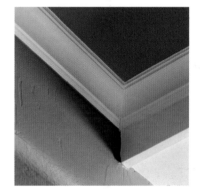
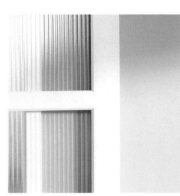

entryways

GLOWING WELCOME. The minute your guests come through the front door, greet them with an entry area that's warm and inviting. One sure way to lighten the mood of any foyer is to paint trimwork white or ivory, then select a wall color that allows a smooth visual transition to adjoining rooms. Even a palette of dark colors won't seem oppressive when paired with the white trim.

DOORS, FLOORS, AND MORE. To enhance transitions consider painting the interior of the front door a different color from the walls, using a second color from the palette of adjoining rooms.

As you plan your entryway palette, consider the floor and ceiling too. The black and white flooring in the entryway *opposite* introduces the black wall and white trim colors in the next room.

Wood flooring warms the entryway *left* while the blue-and-cream harlequin area rug repeats the silvery blue used on the chair cushions.

WELCOMING COMMITTEE
(ABOVE) White paneling keeps the foyer walls looking crisp and clean. Above the paneling soft yellow paint brings warmth to the area. Silvery-hued chairs offer a quiet respite.

WARM WALLS
Russet paint on the walls works with the stained wood elements to make this large entryway cozier. Black and white flooring visually connects the entry to the next room.

RAISED CEILING (ABOVE) To create more volume in the room, the ceiling was raised to 9 feet, which exposed existing beams.

POSITIVE ACCENTS (ABOVE) Glazing the cabinets in a darker color than the white-painted finish tones down the white and gives the room a more vintage appearance.

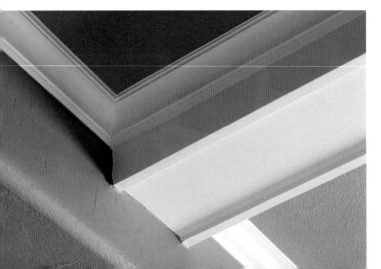

PAINTED POINTS (LEFT) Painting the wooden beams white and then painting the remainder of the ceiling green draws the eye up to the full height of the room. White-painted decorative crown moldings accentuate the connecting point between the wall and ceiling.

kitchens

NATURAL CONNECTION. As discussed in chapter 1, anything you like can inspire a room's color scheme. In this kitchen the sage-green subway tiles were selected for the backsplash and the color plan for the entire room was born.

The color covers the walls, ceiling, backsplash, and island cabinetry. "Painting the walls and the ceilings the same soft color really opens up the space," explains designer Jeremi Headrick. "It makes the room look larger."

CONTINUOUS COLOR. Off-white cabinets warmed by a latte-colored glaze keep the room looking bright and cheerful. Covering the dishwasher and refrigerator with matching cabinetry panels also makes the room appear larger as the soft color flows from wall to wall. Darker, latte-colored ceramic tiles warm the floor. Neutral, speckled black granite covers the countertops.

Because the color design is so simple, Headrick added interest with texture and detail. Walls feature a subtle troweled-on finish that resembles old plaster. Elaborate moldings and trimwork add architectural interest to the cabinets and ceiling.

A simple Roman shade and a few accessories create the only color variations. The shade fabric draws in colors from nearby rooms, creating a visual connection between spaces, while potted plants and vases of fresh flowers underscore the kitchen's natural connection. "It's an easy scheme to duplicate," Headrick says. "And it's a color combination that will never go out of style."

GROUNDED ISLAND (ABOVE) To create more contrast and interest, the island is painted a darker color green than the walls. White trimwork brightens the space.

NEUTRAL TERRITORY
(ABOVE) Stainless-steel sinks and appliances and pewter faucets and fixtures meld with the creamy white of the cabinets and the black of the granite. Dark bronze hardware creates additional color contrast.

RECTILINEAR PATTERN (LEFT)
Laying square tiles on the diagonal and framing the design with pea-shaped trim tiles creates eye-catching pattern behind the cooktop.

color and mood

Cool colors, such as green, blue, and purple, recede into the background, calm nerves, and lift spirits. Neutral colors, such as white, cream, gray, and black, are easy on the eye, promote tranquillity, and work well with other colors.

CLASSIC CONNECTION (LEFT)
The traditional motif of the bright red rug is the only reminder of the kitchen's original classic styling.

NEW ATTITUDE. "Color, finish, and hardware are powerful forces for change," interior designer Barbara Jordan says. And this kitchen makeover proves the point.

Prior to its makeover this kitchen featured soft-white traditional-style cabinets and old-fashioned beaded-board backsplashes. Shiny lacquer paint and industrial-looking hardware transformed the cabinets into the contemporary-looking treasures shown. On the backsplash quilted stainless steel replaces old-fashioned beaded board. The changes make it difficult to tell that this contemporary space was once very traditional in appearance.

Painting the cabinets instead of replacing them left enough money in the budget for a new kitchen island, finished in the same gray color as the cabinets, which complements the charcoal-color granite top. Strategic bursts of bright red and yellow pop out against the sea of gray giving the room a funky 1950s diner feel.

RED BACKING (ABOVE & BELOW) Cabinet interiors kept their classic beaded-board backing, which has been updated with candy-apple red paint. Neon-yellow pendent lamps infuse another flash of primary color.

DINER STYLE (ABOVE) Generous amounts of high-gloss gray lacquer automobile paint and stainless steel infuse this once traditional-style space with industrial edginess and '50s flashbacks.

DESIGN DASH (BELOW)
Combine form with function
by choosing attractive
containers to show off
colorful candies and store
other necessities.

WORK AND PLAY
(LEFT) Make your
workspaces into play
spaces by choosing a
whimsical color scheme
such as the green, blue,
red, and yellow shown.

laundry rooms

PLAYFUL SPIRIT. Coloring your work
spaces in a variety of playful tints and
tones keeps the mood light and the spirit
bright. Start with a random pattern of
colorful tiles on the floors, countertops,
or walls, then transfer the hues to other
surfaces and accessories in the room.

Here the ceramic tile backsplash was
the starting point for this lighthearted
laundry center. Soft green walls create
a soothing surround while colorful
accessories add a fanciful touch.

Vinyl roller shades adorned with floral
bouquets keep dirty clothes baskets
under wraps. A matching floorcloth
adds color underfoot. Painted pegboard
serves as a gift-wrapping center—the
paper and ribbons add even more color. A
shelf above the window is home to more
accessories, including vases and
paper-wrapped storage boxes.

TILE TACTIC (LEFT)
Replacing dated shower tiles with vivid red, orange, and white ones makes the tub area look fresh and new.

bathrooms

EVERYDAY SUNSHINE. Step into your bath and let invigorating colors brighten your day. Warm hues—red, orange, and yellow—energize minds and bodies, brighten moods, and stimulate creativity. They are perfect for a morning wake-up call in the bath, an exercise space, a playroom, or a workshop.

This bath sports bright stripes of red and orange on the walls and a yellow-orange color on the ceiling. White-painted beaded-board wainscoting prevents the wall color from making the small space look too dark and saturated. Red and orange tiles bring additional splashes of color to the tub surround.

ACCESSORY COLOR. For more color fun, bright red bath towels, a mirror with red accents, and framed art depicting a red ladybug adorn the bath.

SHELF EXPRESSION
(LEFT) A white shelf unit coordinates with the beaded board below and provides a place to hang extra towels and display collectibles.

PINING FOR ATTENTION
A pine chest converted
to hold a sink bowl and
plumbing draws attention
to the area. The warmth of
the wood helps balance the
bright colors against the
white floor tiles
and wainscoting.

ETHEREAL PAIR (LEFT) A separate vanity room adjoins the tub and shower area, and puts the emphasis on white-as-a-cloud glass tiles and beaded-board cabinetry. Blue accents, such as the playful glass seahorse knobs and a frosted sink bowl, maintain the visual connection.

BOWLED OVER (BELOW) Blue glass vessel sinks rest on a countertop of white solid-surfacing material speckled with bits of blue glass.

CLEAR VIEW (LEFT) Blue glass tiles continue throughout the shower and all around the tub. The frameless glass shower door ensures an uninterrupted view of the beautiful color.

BLUE RETREAT (ABOVE) Italian glass mosaic tiles climb to the ceiling in this cool blue haven. Copper aggregate embedded in the tile gives it a shimmering water quality.

HEAVENLY
CHOCOLATE (RIGHT)
Sweet dreams are a
sure thing when you
paint bedroom walls
chocolate brown. This
velvety rich color
promotes restfulness
and relaxation.

WILD WALL A lime-green
accent wall breaks up the
brown in the room and draws
attention to the geometric
design of the door when it
is open. The rippled-glass
sliding door ensures privacy
when closed.

bedrooms

CHOCOLATE HUG. Even if you're
resistant to strong color, you may be
willing to embrace dark, bold hues in
the bedroom. Rich color on the walls can
wrap a bedroom like a warm blanket,
making it cozy and calm. This bedroom
is painted a warm, rich brown, which
makes the walls recede and the
furnishings stand out.

COOL ACCENTS. Add light accents to
the dark hue to create a fresh palette.
Splashes of lime green and gold give this
bedroom a fun fashion-forward feel. Plus
gold visually lifts the ceiling and prevents
the room from appearing boxy. Like
black, brown is a neutral and goes with
everything, so it's a great choice when
you are pondering the deep-color plunge.

COLOR COURAGE. If you are nervous
about your decision to paint walls a
deep color, wait until you see the room
with your belongings in place before you
decide. Furnishings, artwork, and white-
painted trim can all make strong color
seem less imposing.

IVORY TOWER

(RIGHT) Multiple shades of white and cream create an airy, restful feel for this bedroom. Various materials on the bed and at the window lend textural interest.

RETRO ACTIVE

(LEFT) If you ever tote home a vintage 1950s bed, complete with sliding headboard, take a cue from this setting and top it with mod-style bedding. This spread and shams feature a burnt-orange and cream design that's a definite blast from the past.

RASPBERRY RESPITE (ABOVE) Mottled reddish-pink wall color provides a luscious backdrop for the white French bed with sage-green accents. Beside the bed an antique rug repeats versions of the wall hue and introduces refreshing touches of lemon yellow.

children's bedrooms

STAR QUALITY (ABOVE) Deep blue walls serve as a night sky stage for the dancing figures in Collier's bedroom. "I like the way the stars are painted," she says. "They aren't pointy like other stars; they help me relax."

NURTURE IMAGINATION. A stimulating environment fosters a stimulating child—that's artist Landen Summay's theory behind the brightly painted bedrooms he creates for young people of all ages.

The idea blossomed when he and Pam Green wanted "to do something special" in their daughters' bedrooms. For inspiration in 7-year-old Lola's room, Summay took his cue from a flower-shape rug, wrapping the room in a joyful mix of bright blue, apple green, lavender, and sunny yellow. Spirals, flowers, and flowing ribbons of white float across the walls and ceiling, creating an atmosphere of wonder and activity. "I like the way all the flowers use different colors," Lola says.

Collier, 9, enjoys a room of Matisse-type movement where stylized green and red figures dance in spotlights blazing through fields of bold blue. It's the stars that twinkle across the tops of the walls and across the ceiling that she loves best though.

SPUNKY SPIRALS (BELOW) Spirals adapted from a flower-shape rug bring delightful pattern to the room.

FLOWER POWER In Lola's room the ceiling fixture becomes part of the painted design where a pinwheel of color swirls with the fan blades.

GARDEN VARIETY Blue tile facing the fireplace and sunny yellow walls welcome the bouquet of character and color introduced by this courageous mix of fabric patterns.

PATTERN PLAYS
(ABOVE) Florals and
awninglike stripes work
together to bring an
outdoor feel inside.

living rooms

OPPORTUNITY KNOCKS. Though guests
gain their first impression from your home's
entryway, the living room can be the space
where they spend more time and can
discover the colors and style you love. Use
this space as a canvas for creating a mood
that's vibrant and active or subdued and
relaxed. Express your love of bold primary
colors and contemporary style or bestow
garden charm with florals and stripes.

QUIET ELEGANCE (LEFT) Silvery blues and grays and subtle champagne touches make this conversation group gracious but relaxed. Painting the fireplace surround white establishes it as the room's focus without screaming for attention.

FURNITURE FLAIR (BELOW) Brightly painted furniture plays a key role in this joyfully decorated living room. Located lakeside, the cottage is meant for fun, and the lively colors emphasize the casual lifestyle.

PATTERN PLAYS (ABOVE) Toile and gingham pillows present color with charm in this cottage-style living room. Covering the upholstered furnishings with white slipcovers invites any combination of hues into the space.

MIDSUMMER MAGIC (BELOW) When you lavish a room in layers of white, you're assured of a setting that always feels sunny and airy—even in the dead of winter. Combine any number of shades of white for variety and mix in textural elements for more interest.

MOD SQUAD (ABOVE) Modern furnishings show off their shapely lines dressed in green, white, and black. Oversize artwork adds drama.

SUNNY SHADES Warm golds combine with black and mahogany accents to create an inviting ambience.

dining
rooms

COLORS TO REMEMBER. Make every meal memorable by creating a dining room that's as enticing as the food you serve and as captivating as the conversation. Here are some color ideas to enhance your dining experience:

- **Red** is said to stimulate conversation as well as appetites. To prevent red from appearing too intense, which can make white linens appear dull, select a red with blue or brown undertones.
- **Orange,** like the fruit, is packed with energy. You'll find any of its variations—apricot and peach to melon, carrot, and pumpkin—can warm up your guests and grab their attention.
- **Green** conjures images of nature and promotes health and well-being. Today green is considered a neutral color that works with any hue.
- **Blue,** although said to reduce appetite, also encourages harmony and tranquillity.
- **Purple** can be used to create an exotic setting or an environment that makes everyone feel regal. It is a color for passionate people and purposeful conversations.
- **Yellow** can make your dining room appear sunny on the cloudiest day, ensuring that your guests feel joyful and optimistic.
- **White,** with its connections to purity and cleanliness, can be a stress-reliever. Used in abundance white instills a sense of airiness and calm.
- **Black** suggests elegance and formality. A few black accents lend sophistication to almost any color scheme.

PEACEFUL WHITE
(ABOVE) You can almost feel the breeze wafting through this airy dining room. The brick floor and wooden tabletop ground the neutrals in warm tones.

NATURE CALLS (BELOW) Citrus accents of lemon yellow and persimmon add zing to this garden-inspired breakfast room. The huge philodendron leaves on the table and chairs were cut from a roll of wallpaper and decoupaged to the painted wood pieces.

SHERBET SENSATIONS (ABOVE) A wood table and chairs could have been humdrum but seem adventurous and fun when dressed in blue and purple. Runners are blue silk banded in green, visually connecting the table to the seating as well as the low side table beneath the window.

OFFICE OPPORTUNITY (LEFT) In this office built-in laminate storage and wood flooring serve as neutral territory for setting off a stylish set of orange chairs.

bonus spaces

HOUSETOP HAVEN (BELOW) Pale sage walls with white woodwork and white on the sloping ceiling prevent this under-the-eaves bathroom from feeling cramped.

IMAGINE THIS. Attics, basements, unused bedrooms, porches and sunrooms, and above-the-garage quarters all offer one thing in common—extra space for hobbies, home offices, playrooms, and music rooms, to name only a few possibilities. And whether your bonus space will be bursting with activity or designated for quiet concentration, you can find a color mix to fit your frame of mind. Consider shades of green for a home office, for example, to reduce stress and keep your mind clear. In a child's playroom, encourage creativity with a batch of crayon colors on walls and furnishings. For an artist's studio repeat the hues of your favorite painting all around the room. You have only one rule: Let your imagination reign.

SOOTHING SANCTUM
A combination of greens provides a low-stress environment for working at home. Lighter shades prevent the space from appearing sleepy while dashes of orange add visual spice; wood tones lend warmth.

HIGH-STYLE SUNPORCH. Although the designer of this porch had originally thought about a blue-and-yellow combination, the homeowners decided to restore it to the 1907 open-air style. The new black-and-white color palette began when a quest for furniture yielded the black rattan sofa and chairs. Crisp white acrylic curtain panels pair with white cushions and black-and-white pillows to give the new outdoor living space a turn-of-the-century high-style look. Splashes of red finish the porch with pizzazz.

BASIC BORDER (BELOW) The black hook-and-loop tape border visually links the fabric panels to the room design and also allows the panels to fasten together for privacy and protection from the elements.

CLASSIC REVIVAL Hardy furnishings, an outdoor rug, acrylic fabrics, and durable accessories allow this sunporch to function as an outdoor living area.

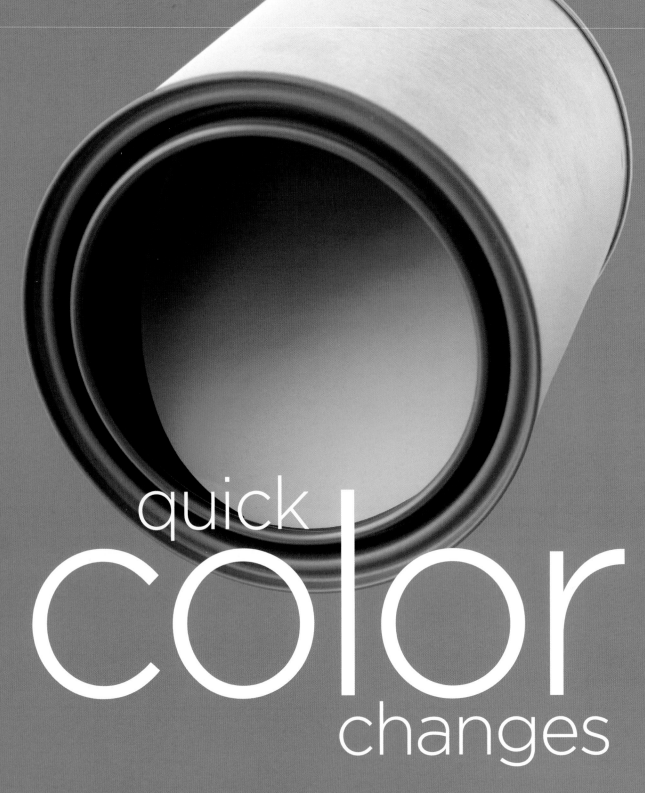

quick color changes

Do you simply love a rainbow of colors and want to enjoy a varying palette throughout the year? Or are you working up the courage to incorporate color into your home? Whichever scenario describes you these ideas will let you change color schemes without a lot of fuss.

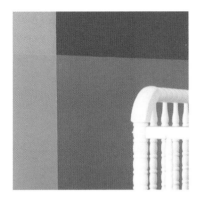
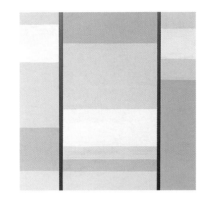
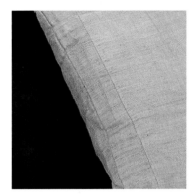

painted transformations

BLOCKBUSTER STYLE. Paint is one of the most inexpensive decorating tools around, making a big impact on a space for a small amount of money. The time you invest depends on the size of the surface you plan to paint and the intricacy of the project. Though the multicolored blocked wall in the bedroom *opposite* might take a weekend to create, the wall squares, painted canvases, and painted chairs in the dining room *right* could be completed individually in an afternoon. Either way you don't have to be afraid of color mistakes because your costs to repaint are minimal.

If you decide to paint one or more walls in a room, let the paint dry before making a final judgment; paint color always looks different when it's wet.

Remember that you can tame even the most dramatically hued wall by positioning furniture in front of it or hanging artwork on it. The white linens and white furnishings in these two rooms lend visual balance to the bold colors.

BLOCKBUSTER MAKEOVER (RIGHT) For a quick transformation, make three-dimensional color blocks on walls. Outline blocks with painter's tape to ensure crisp edges. Top with canvases painted in solid colors. Finish the treatment with painted chairs.

INSIDE THE LINES
Vibrant color blocks, created by masking off squares with painter's tape, transform these bedroom walls into a graphic celebration of purple and blue.

FAST FLIP (LEFT) A trio of painted closet doors forms this colorful headboard. Paint each side with a different palette to complement seasonal linens. Then flip the doors when you're ready for a change.

BLACK IN BACK
(LEFT) Blackboard paint provides the neutral yet dramatic backdrop for the colors to come in this kitchen. Artwork and flowers introduce more easy-change color.

SOUPED-UP SISAL
(ABOVE) Customize a plain sisal rug with a freehand flower or use stamps or stencils to apply a design. This flower was applied with acrylic paints and a stiff brush.

NEW HEIGHTS (ABOVE AND RIGHT) Applying color to the lower portion of a white wall—just below a chair rail molding—is a fast way to enliven a plain space. Black and white artwork and lampshades add contemporary punch and will work with whatever color chair cushions you choose. Change the cushions to change the mood of the room.

soft touches

TEXTILE TRICKS. Fabrics and other soft touches can easily be moved into and around a room for flexible color options. Here are only a few ideas:

- **Accent pillows** are the perfect tool to add fresh color to your decor. Mix and match colors and patterns and toss decorative pillows onto chairs, sofas, the bed, and even the floor. If you spot a pillow or two that might or might not work, go ahead and buy them. Unlike a sofa, they're relatively inexpensive and simple to return.

- **Window treatments**, such as rod pocket and tie-top panels, are simple to slide on and off a rod to give a window—and the entire room—a new look.

- **Slipcovers.** Old, faded upholstered furniture or plain pieces dress up in alternative hues and patterns when you top them with slipcovers. When the fabric becomes soiled or you're ready for another color, switch to a new cover and toss the old one in the washer.

PILLOW POWER (LEFT)
Power-up a taupe sofa with a punch of today's hot hue. The little jolt of color offered by accent pillows can reinforce a focal point or complement artwork and other accessories in the room.

SHOWERED IN COLOR (ABOVE) For a custom shower curtain, fashion a panel from fabric you like and team it with a purchased clear plastic shower curtain liner. Line the top edge with grommets for threading on shower curtain rings or use clip-on rings.

FLOOR SHOW (LEFT)
Make a conversation group cohesive with a rug that pulls together all the colors of your palette. Start with neutral furnishings and switch to different colored rugs on a whim.

FABRIC FLEXIBILITY
(ABOVE) Stroll through a fabric store and imagine the possibilities. Consider coordinating fabrics for a duvet, pillow shams, and a bed skirt for quick-change color options in the bedroom, for example.

GOOD THROW (LEFT) Neutral upholstered furnishings earn a dash of color when a throw of autumn colors is casually draped over the ottoman. Purchase a throw for every season (rich hues for fall and winter and light colors for spring and summer) and make this simple switch whenever the weather turns.

COZY HEADBOARD (LEFT) Freshen a bed frame with a fabric slipcover that ties in place. Make it reversible for a new look to match a different set of linens.

SLIP SHAPE To create a cottage or antique-style room, look for vintage fabrics for fashioning slipcovers for upholstered furniture, such as this chair and ottoman.

SWITCHABLE SHADES (ABOVE)
Top a lamp with a fabric shade in a hue that complements your room's color palette. Add fringe, cording, or beaded trim to the bottom edge for additional color.

TRIM TRICK Add architectural interest instantly to a room and beef up your color palette by securing ribbon to walls as shown. Wherever ribbons crisscross, use a decorative-head thumbtack to secure the lengths and introduce more color. Tuck colorful postcards and photographs behind the ribbon.

PRINTS CHARMING
(LEFT) Botanical prints hung above this bathtub inject bolder hues into the quiet decor. Discount books can often yield affordable prints that can be slipped into the same set of frames when you want a change.

TABLE CHIC (LEFT) Start with a white or neutral tablecloth and then pull out complementary colored plates and cloth napkins, placemats, and napkin rings to make a dramatic statement. Mix and match dishware, glassware, and linens for a different look every time.

art & accessories

SMALL WONDERS. Stroll through the aisles of The Home Depot®, department stores, discount stores, flea markets, and garage sales to find endless options for adding color using art and accessories. Because these items are generally small and portable, they're simple to relocate around a room or rotate in and out of storage. Here are just a few ideas to prime your imagination:

▸ Top the table with lively placemats, pottery, or a tray of vases.

▸ Bring collections into the limelight and group pieces by color for dramatic impact.

▸ Brighten shelves with stacks of books, handpainted plates, colorfully framed photos, and colored glass bottles.

▸ Paint inexpensive picture frames for splashes of wall-hung color.

▸ Purchase outdated calendars featuring artwork you love. Frame your favorites and change out the images whenever you find others you want to enjoy.

▸ Show off colorful and edible fare, such as strawberry wafers, brightly wrapped candies, and dried pastas in clear glass canisters or bowls.

BATH BEAUTIFIERS (BELOW) Colored bath oils and liquid soaps stored in clear glass bottles become beautiful accessories when displayed on an open shelf or inside a glass cabinet. Assorted towels in multiple hues enhance the scheme.

A wide and colorful selection of pendent fixtures and table and floor lamps is available. Shaded ceiling fixtures, such as these above the dining table, require only a few hours to install. Or simply switch the shade on any style of fixture to gain fresh color, pattern, and texture.

COLLECTIVE THOUGHTS
(ABOVE) An open set of
shelves becomes a display
space for these collectible
water pitchers.

nature's bounty

HARVEST OF HUES. Farmer's markets, your own backyard, florists, and even the supermarket can be gold mines of changeable color. Flowers, fruit, vegetables, plants, and other greenery are fair game for splashing color in every room of the house. For dramatic impact go with all one color. Or create a mix of colors from nature that complements fabrics or other items in the room. The container in which you display the bounty is still as important. Select clear or white bowls, trays, or vases when you want the natural elements to be the focus. For added visual flair, choose containers in colors that complement the blooms or produce you want to display.

ROSY DINING (ABOVE)
Give an all-white dining room a fresh face by varying tabletop decor. Here fresh-from-the-garden tulips combine with pink shawls used as table runners.

FRUITFUL LIVING If you love change choose an adaptable color scheme. Coffee, black, and white can mix and match with almost any color. Then accessorize with trendy accent colors, such as these lime-green pillows and citrus-green pears.

BRANCHING OUT (LEFT & ABOVE) The tabletop is the perfect place to display your color choice of the day. This bouquet of branches bedecked in bold red leaves serves as an eyecatching centerpiece that nature provided free of charge. Gathered around the vase are colorful miniature gourds and squashes.

WALL FLOWERS (ABOVE) A wall with handpainted blossoms springs to life with fresh flowers, sprigs of ferns, and fragrant herbs in clear vases. Shop flea markets and garage sales to find unique platforms for hanging the vases, such as this hat rack.

PRESSED POSIES (RIGHT) For more changeable color place a few colorful decorations between stacks of two clear glass plates. Pansies, photographs, postcards, and wrapping paper are simply a few items that work wonders.

contact information

The Home Depot® offers paint and materials from major manufacturers either in stock or through special order. Information on products and materials can be obtained from design centers in Home Depot stores or directly through manufacturers by mail, telephone, or online.

Contacting Meredith Corporation
To order this and other Meredith Corporation books call 800/678-8091. For further information about the material contained in this book, please contact Meredith by e-mail at hi123@mdp.com or by phone at 800/678-2093.

Contacting The Home Depot®
For general information about product availability contact your local Home Depot or visit The Home Depot® website at www.homedepot.com.

resources

Listed below are the names of the professionals who worked on the locations featured exclusively in *The Home Depot® Color Designs for Living.* You can find these locations on pages 104, 108–115, 122–129, 138–141, and 154–155.

Colors

Please be aware that paint colors shown in the book may look different on your wall because of the printing process used in this book. If you see a color you like, show it to a Home Depot associate in the paint department, and he or she will custom-tint paint to match it as closely as possible. Buy samples of paint in small quantities and test areas so that you can see the result prior to spending time and money to paint the entire room. Changes in lighting affect colors, which, for instance, can seem remarkably different under artificial light and natural light. Paint a test area and live with it under different lighting conditions for at least 24 hours to make sure it is right for you. Also, consult everyone who will be living with the color.

page 105

Interior designer: Edwin Pepper Interiors
Photographer: Alise O'Brien

pages 108–115

Interior designer: Iliana Moore, Columbine Antiques & Decorations Ltd., Bronxville, New York; 917/689-1937; www.centerart.com
Photographer: Michael Partenio Productions
Field editor: Karin Lidbeck-Brent

pages 122–129

Interior designer: Suzanne Radi, Suzanne Radi Designs Ltd., Wilmette, IL 60091; 847/256-1364
Photographer: Janet Mesic Mackie
Field editor: Hillary Rose

pages 138–141

Architect: Michael Lyons, AIA, Dallas, TX 75234; 214/256-9600
Interior designers: Pamela Jackson and Jeremi Headrick; Jackson Vaughn, McKinney, Texas; 972/529-9339
Photographer: Dan Piassick
Field editor: Diane Carrol

pages 154–155

Artist: Landen Summay, Groovenile Environments, Cincinnati, Ohio; 513/871-4518; www.groovenile.com
Photographer: Tony Walsh
Field editor: Kelly Watts

index

a

b

c–d

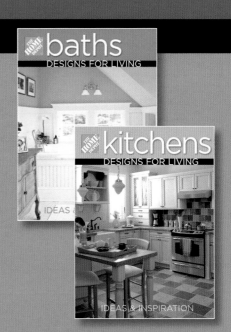